WELLSPRINGS

poems by

Elizabeth Shafer

Finishing Line Press
Georgetown, Kentucky

WELLSPRINGS

For Stephen, and for the rest of my family, who helped me love,
for Hongnian Zhang, who helped me paint,
and for teachers like Julia McGrew, who helped me love poems
by Donne, Blake, Dickenson, Levertov, and other poets

ACKNOWLEDGMENTS

With thanks for the friendship and advice of Bo Niles; and for the inspiration
and guidance of Hughie Lee-Smith, my painting teacher at the Art Students
League; Ansei Uchima, my woodblock printing teacher at Columbia
University School of the Arts; Cynthia Winika, my encaustic teacher at the
R&F Studios; Kate McGloughlin, my printmaking teacher at the Woodstock
School of Art; Yu Chen Chao, my cello teacher; and Peter Weiss, John
Burroughs, Alyn Ware, and Anabel Dwyer, my colleagues at the Lawyers'
Committee on Nuclear Policy.

Publisher: Leah Maines
Editor: Christen Kincaid
Cover Encaustic & Inner Woodcuts: Elizabeth Shafer
Author Photo: Stephen Shafer
Cover Design: Elizabeth Maines McCleavy

Printed in the USA on acid-free paper.
Order online: www.finishinglinepress.com
also available on amazon.com

Author inquiries and mail orders:
Finishing Line Press
P. O. Box 1626
Georgetown, Kentucky 40324
U. S. A.

Table of Contents

I. MÈRE

Matrix Web

Your low slow voice, your dark sloe-eyed gaze,
vague, distant, doe-like, your shoulders curving
like your combs you let me stroke through waves
of your thick black hair while you sang, preserving
nighttime rites of lullabies. In shafts of late sun, coils
of cigarette smoke unfurled as you brushed
pigments on canvas with turpentine, linseed oil,
and with a whiff of gin, your talk was hushed.
Divorced, you married again and moved away, then
I married young, and from a distance, heard
that you fell asleep and died, asphyxiated, when
your cigarette fell in sofa folds, other facts blurred.
Decades ago, your spirit left before you left,
and I am left with strands, caught in time's weft.

Invisible Indivisible Bonds

When your long lovely form was first laid on my chest
where your head with its shock of dark hair knocked,
my heart knocked at the sight of your dark eyes staring
and your bud-like mouth rooting for my breast.
The fibrous sanguine cord that had bound us
in my womb had been cut, but
deep invisible links continued to bind us
when I took you, my daughter and first-born child,
home. I was mostly alone with you that first year
since your father began as a medical intern
the day you were born. But my tension turned to peace
when I felt my womb's rhythmic tug while nursing you.
One day when you were two, we joined
a friend and her little girl in Riverside Park.
We strapped you in seats in the back of our bikes
and rode toward the Boat Basin, whizzing
with the wind past trees and park gardens,
our wheels on the pavement thrumming,
my elation rising as I heard you humming
along with the wind while you leaned against me
and I felt currents between us vibrating.

Later that year your brother was born
and the next four years seemed filled
with happy hectic days, until dark clouds
unaccountably closed in on me like shrouds
and I had to leave you and stay on a ward
for months, while longing to see, hold and hug you
and your brother, with phone calls
and occasional visits our only links.

Yet when I finally came home
I felt the bond I'd built with you
over the past six years had stayed
strong and true.
When you were eight, your sister was born
and you were happy playing with her
and your brother; you also were adept
at balancing with grace
the ambiguities of disparate worlds:

living with your parents on the West Side
of Manhattan; visiting your grandfather
at his spacious country estate; but
I sometimes felt I strained our bond
by leaning on you, my first child,
inaptly as a friend and confidante.

And I wasn't fully aware of the strains
you faced during your teenage years:
the lure of drugs, sex, alcohol; the fear
and extent of AIDS. One weekend night
you said you'd join friends in the Village
and I asked you to phone us if you'd be home
after 1 a.m. At 2 a.m. you phoned
with some reasons: you'd had trouble finding
a phone booth (a time before mobile phones);
you'd lost money for a cab or subway tokens;
a strap on one of your sandals broke; but you said
you were walking barefoot up Broadway toward home.
In fear and fondness I imagined you with the beauty
of your face and form, walking
barefoot in the dark the ninety blocks north;
but glad of the sound of your voice
through links, though tenuous, of phone lines.

As a young woman, you were focused and fervent
about human rights: helping immigrants
find sanctuary at Las Americas in El Paso;
in your work as deputy representative
of Amnesty International to the U.N;
or as asylum program officer for clients
at a law firm whose mission was human rights.
Your care for global human suffering
was linked but distinct
from mine on nuclear issues
and far less abstract.

Fervent in love as well as work,
you married a man with kindred views, but
a few years later, depression struck

you, in a cruel recurrent way:
lifting to joy with the birth of your first
child, a wonderful little boy;
turning to shock and grief with the birth
of your second child, a stillborn son;
then turning back to joy with the birth
of a healthy child, another amazing son;
and then a daughter, a beautiful little girl.
Having a great spouse too; having had depression too,
losing a baby too, before the joy of having you,
I've felt linked with you in sadnesses and joys.
And now, in your middle years and my late ones
I celebrate our invisible indivisible bonds.

in a city apartment", and you countered
logically and insistently, "but cats don't have
to go outside." And when we still demurred,
you searched through animal shelters, then said
"I've found a cat who's been lost, abandoned
and probably abused." You brought
her home, and took protective and loving
care of her.

When you grew up and moved away
to college, then to work where you explored
the allure for you of public radio,
then to grad school, you had
your own apartment where you brought
cats from shelters: one ill and nervous,
the other toothless, needing soft food.
Both needy, you responded to each
with loving care.

Now, adept and savvy about
technical aspects of digital audio files,
you produce podcasts on important
and complex social issues.
In your life you've moved far beyond
your childhood focus on cats. And now
you plan to have a dog also.
But sometimes I recall how
when you were about ten, you brought

a homeless cat home, and I feel
this reflects some admirable traits
you share with cats:
independent, enigmatic, fanciful, loving.
And whenever I think of you, I'm filled
with great pride as well as deep
love for you.

Belle Mère

'Belle Mère': beautiful mother;
French words lovelier
than the legalistic English term
'mother-in-law', and
far more fitting for you, dear M
and who you were for me
from the time I first glimpsed
your wide smile, your slim form
so like your son's, whom I also met
that distant August night when I fell
instantly in love with him—and also
with you, when you opened
your home and heart to me that autumn
and the next four years while
S and I fell deeper in love.

I was in awe of your myriad
talents: as a writer, piano teacher
and other roles, though a mere listing
of these could never embrace
your ineffable vibrant spirit,
your love's magnetic force
encompassing
the depth of family love,
the breadth of friendship,
the complexity of sex.

During the four years after
S and I married, you
were my friend and confidante,
like a sister or mother
after the sudden death
of my birth mother.
And for years after
our children were born
you helped with their care
as their fun and loving Grandma
whom they loved to visit
where you read and told them stories
and they danced to music

as you played the piano.
"Splendid," you'd say, responding
to all efforts with your spirited
message: to expect the best
of oneself, but that trying
was what mattered most.
And when you listened
to family members or friends
you made each person feel
that she or he was then
the only person
in the world for you.

Then why did I cause
discord and distance
to grow between us
from resentments
and misunderstandings?
My petty, passive-aggressive
attitude, actions, words
stab and twist in me
with their memories, and
my futile longing
to undo them.

Since you've died, though,
I've broached my remorse
about this with
your younger daughter, who said
"Mother would have liked you
to look forward, not back."
And we talked about a new film,
"Pay it Forward," with the theme
from an old book, *In the Garden
of Delight*: "you don't pay love back,
you pay it forward." And since then
I feel that my sisters-in-law
have become my belles soeurs.

Yet memories still rush back:

your welcoming touch of leaving
books like *Friend of my Youth*
by Alice Munro, a fellow writer whose work
with its exotic twists you valued,
on our bedside table when we visited you.
Or your hopeful breathless eager voice
on your answering machine:
"Tell me something I don't know."

And though it may be just
a wishful hope that love is like
the fragile but recurrent flowering
of perennial plants in spring,
I long to have you know how I wish
I could erase the darkness I caused
between us, and return to those years
of light and youth and love,
my beautiful mother, sister, and friend.

II. WELLSPRINGS

Some Joy

"Looking for joy, some joy/ not to be found outside it"
—from "The Ache of Marriage," Denise Levertov

Alone together
rapt wrapped,
twisting
in whorls
up
from some
deep undersea
tumult
erupting cresting
subsiding
in rippling pulsing
currents

Ecstasy
flowing together
in dancelike trance
with a joyful sense
of our oneness

Ekstasis
standing apart
with different interests
the ache of awareness
of our separateness.

Together with you
during
the rollercoaster
of those years
when our lives
were meshed
with the knotted
cries and laughter
of our children
playing, fighting,
swinging
back to uncertain peace.

Joy in watching
our children grow,
the need for accord
to care for their needs

Friction from discord
on ways to raise them,
ephemeral longings
for other lovers

Together alone
with you
now all three children
are grown
and living away

I remember those years
of bedtime readings,
trips to the park, vacations,
picnics, birthday parties
and other times
of joy, warmth, laughter
bursting like sun or
rippling like water

I try to cast away
the ache of memories
of varied hurts
that I incurred
those that don't "lie
too deep for tears"
yet somehow stay
unsaid, unshed

I reach my hand
across our bed
beyond my tears
to stroke your arm
across the years
and find you there

again I stretch my hand
and find you here.

Ekphrases: Four Paintings by C. F. S.
1855-1925

A canvas tiny as a postcard
limns, in thick
diminutive daubs,
tan sands, reddish rocks
jutting back toward a grove
of scrubby pines, lining
the shore of an ocean cove
where two boats—one with full
wide-spreading white sails—float
in seawater whose hue,
a clear cerulean blue—
all seem as though
this small quick oil sketch
was for you
simply a souvenir
of a day when joy
was deep as the sea
and vast as the sky.

A canvas where nearby tall pines
set the scale, but these are towering ones
with just the top branches visible
in the foreground: your site
on a craggy wooded road, or
some other rough terrain of vast height.
Below another wooded crag
a tiny hull of a distant boat
drifts in the green-blue cove
of an alpine lake. Above
the jagged shoreline, small white houses
are notched into hillsides, and beyond,
violet snow-capped mountains rise
high into a blue cloudless sky.

A painting of a little girl, her dark eyes
looking up from the pages
of an open book that rests
on the lap of her yellow dress,
her inquiring gaze

with her up-tilted cleft chin,
the limber shape of her small frame
set among pillows in a velvet chair,
happily lost in the pages of her book,
as only those long summer hours
of childhood can bring, she's just now
been drawn from it, to pose.
And so she sits, pensive, winsome:
my father's sister Lizzie as a young girl.

                    Three   roses   whose
                    lemon-yellow petals
                                        unfold
                              above
                                        the
                                        curving
                              handle
                    of a silver chalice
                    embossed with scalloped
                    beads of grapes, its rounded
                    curve overlaid with a thick white
                    highlight, glowing from an ink-blue
                              backdrop, with
                              scrolled lines
                              of the vase
                              tapering
                              down
                              to
                              a
                    thin base on
                    olive-green ground:
            'nature morte', yet it seems more 'tableau vivant',
                    blooming, looming out from the darkness.

Paternal Patterns

On walks sometimes your hands reached down to hold
my little sister's hand, and mine, to press
the pattern of our silent code, and fold
us in fond queries. "Do you love me?" "Yes,"

"I do." "How much?" Brief squeeze between each word,
then, a long firm squeeze. A way to keep in touch
while we lived with our mother, distance blurred
by divorce, and we could not see you as much.

In summers when we stayed with you we rode,
cantering over sunlit fields quilted with ponds
into deep woods. In the hush our pace slowed
to a trot, as a thrush called among fern fronds.

Behind your house was a garden of curved
symmetries: knot beds, clipped and rounded trees,
a pergola arched with vines, its curve conserved,
peacocks' fan-tailed flaunting, gliding down with ease.

Lunch *al fresco* while we perched on upturned glazed
Chinese urns; afternoons reading while sunlight stayed;
dinner prompt on silver plates after restful days
patterned with the help of grooms, gardeners, maids.

One year, trying to keep your mind and hands full
while you stopped smoking, you took up needlepoint,
guiding through tiny holes long threads of wool,
intricate rugs and pillows the endpoint.

Another year I often saw you pore
over Arrighi's *Operina*, transcribed
by Benson on calligraphy, the core:
cursive writing you practiced like a scribe.

Sometimes I watched you hold a strand of beads
your fingers moving over each, your lips
moving as you murmured rosary creeds:
Hail Mary, Our Father, and other prayerful scripts.

Your Catholic faith, with structure like your past
naval service, was strong, but patterns in your life
became a blur for me at eighteen, cast
shade on my sexual stirrings, filled with strife.

Your ordered life seemed far as a snow globe,
frozen in the past, when I married young and
joy turned to shock at deaths, wanting to probe
my mother's; news of King's, and those in Vietnam.

But when I brought our children to visit you,
you fondly doted on them, gave them treats
like pony rides and carriage drives, but they knew
your values were greater than any sweets.

Yet I could not deny the split I felt
between your family love and apparent views
praising women as wives and mothers, that dealt
them strict roles instead of those they might choose.

My loss as much as yours that distance grew:
you, adhering to strict Catholicism,
I to liberal humanism, but true
and open talks could have lessened schisms.

Your lawyer was your lifelong friend who chose
as his successor someone who made choices cursed
by failure, so your dreams for your estate froze
after you died, and your vast wealth dispersed.

I knew some sadnesses in your past: the deaths
of your parents, brother, and first-born child, before
your divorce. She died two weeks after her first breaths,
and on your birthday, facts that shook me to the core.

Now, remembering your losses and your gifts
I wish I could reach my hand across the years
to press yours, in patterns healing rifts:
"Do you love me?' "Yes I do," with joy, not tears.

Sisterly Synergy

I remember how
when we were little girls
we'd often run together
at bedtime down the long hall
to your bedroom, where I'd say
"I'm putting you to bed," but then
you'd run back with me down the hall
to my bedroom, where you'd say
"I'm putting *you* to bed now!" We'd laugh
and turn and run together
down the hall: back and forth
unwilling to let each other go.

You're only sixteen months younger
and though we had sibling spats:
(I recall with chagrin how, admiring
the full-throated song of your canary,
I tricked you into trading him
for a pile of comic books!) an act
that I hope was reversed
and short-lived, like our other spats.
And good times prevailed, like our sharing
the care of our mop-like mutt Spot.

Too little to remember
when our mother divorced our father,
we stayed at our mother's apartment
most of the time, and went
to our father's country place
summers and some weekends.

Tensions from this split life
took their toll: each of us
developed a sporadic
but debilitating stutter:
the mind forms thoughts
that need to be voiced
with clarity, but the choice
of certain words causes
the throat to shut, the tongue

and lips to turn numb,
the thoughts blocked,
the speaker locked.
You and I shared
this tacit misery for years.

But time and the wider world
lessened this impediment:
we were fortunate
in our school, which nurtured
curiosity and creativity
in a classical curriculum.
You excelled in science
and arithmetic, while I,
drawn more to art and poetry,
admired your analytical mind.
Our paths and choices diverged
as we grew up: you became
a Catholic with strong faith
while I remained Episcopalian
with deep doubts. We went
to different colleges, after which
you joined a science team in Antarctica
then entered a pre-med program.

I married young, painted,
had two daughters and a son,
struggled through law school.
You went to med school,
married, had two sons,
and trained to be a surgeon,
overcoming male bias against
women in your chosen field.

My sister a surgeon!
I was in awe, imagining
your thin form bending
over your patients, your hand
holding a scalpel, your long fingers
gently but adeptly probing

and sewing up their wounds,
working long hours with the weight
of knowledge that you had
the lives of your patients
literally in your hands.

And now when I consult new doctors
and they ask my family history,
I mention you, and I'm proud
but not surprised when they say
"Oh, I trained with her!" or "I refer
patients to her—a wonderful doctor!"

Now we're the only people in the world
who've known each other all our lives,
since our parents and most relatives have died,
so though our traits and lives may differ,
our shared childhood forms
our deep and unique bond
of sisterly synergy.

III. VORTEX

Haiku, and Horror

Etsuko showed me calm
in the white stones combed around
black rocks at Ryoan-ji

                radioactive
        into a   cloud
        turning   spreading
        then   radioactive
        sky   dust
        in the   far and wide
        high   falling down
        rising   to earth

            of the sun
        as the center
            hot
        a fireball
        blast then
        a massive
            First
then terror children women men running
skin burnt blackened crying water water
radiation sickness thyroid cancers in children
lingering through time across space

Dominion

"And God said, Let...man...
have dominion over all the earth."   —Genesis I, 26

As a child, taken
to the Barnum and Bailey circus,
I was excited by all the sights
like the graceful but perilous acts
of tightrope walkers and trapeze artists,
the blare of trombones and brass bands,
aromas from cones of candy cotton,
the musky smells from animal pens
from where tigers and elephants were led
in procession into the ring.
The trainers cracked their whips,
as the elephants rose on pedestals,
then slowly knelt,
the tigers leapt through flaming hoops.
Ignorant of the wrongness of these acts
I was also drawn to the lure of a souvenir:
a tiny turtle, its back shellacked,
sold in a matchbox.
And I was taken too
to the Central Park Zoo,
where we walked around
the dingy grey space, I cajoling
for the popcorn and peanut
caramel-coated treat
of Crackerjacks, oblivious
to the trapped, forlorn looks
of monkeys and other animals
pacing in their cages.

But my outlook changed
as the world changed:
fewer bees, frogs, butterflies
from DDT and other toxic sprays,
birds, spiders, reindeer
poisoned by radiation,
snow leopards, giant pandas,
Asian elephants endangered
by habitat loss and poaching,

plankton and corals
made acid, bleached,
sea lions, penguins, walruses,
threatened by oil spills and plastic trash,
polar bears alone and adrift
on icebergs melting
from heat and rising seas,
these dire facts made more stark
By glossy photographs in magazines.

Dazed, numbed, shocked
by the enormity of these,
I try to make changes in my life:
drive less, walk more,
eat less meat or fish, then none,
though aware how paltry
and inconsequential my efforts are.
Yet wanting to have these seem
less abstract and extreme,
I go with our grandson Reid
to the Central Park Zoo, newly
improved: a snow leopard leaping
among rocks in a cage-less habitat,
and with lines from nature poems
carved in stone steps.
Later, Reid's little sister Isabelle gazes
cross-eyed with awe at a caterpillar
perched on her finger, and at our farm she puts
carcasses of ladybugs in boxes, hoping
to coax them back to life.

And I think of the tall thin thoughtful leader
who held out a slim ray of hope for the world
by urging the Paris Climate Accord,
after the callow Boy-King chief
spurned climate accords
of Rio and Kyoto, and before
the current Clod-in-Chief
quashed most hope.

Now I see new photographs
of polar bears, not only
alone and adrift
on melting icecaps,
but also starving,
and I wonder if Reid, Isabelle,
and our other grandchildren
will have a world worth living for.

Bulldozed

The big blond-headed bull
blunders around the china shop
smashing the fragile stems
of glasses holding
people's hopes and dreams.

He bellows against those
who don't look or act like him,
trying to ban them from traveling
or invading his turf, and vows
to build a border wall
to keep them out. He condones
separating calves
from their parent cows,
oblivious to longterm harms
to young calves kept in cages
and their anguished parent cows.

He hulks and lumbers
after alluring nubile heifers,
pressing his massive bulk on them.
When they demur, he brays
"Never happened" when questioned.
His contempt for questioning females
is not confined to calves: "Miss Piggy",
"Dog", "Horseface."

Too obtuse to use logic, he deals in tweets.
"Climate change? a hoax," he huffs.
"Nuclear weapons?" he snorts:
"If we have them, why not use them?"

The hand writing this
stops. Why
should I try
to write a poem when art,
truth, and fairness
are dead?

"Her ass meant

to me two golden globes
encased in her jeans
I'd like to hold in my hands
like her soft firm breasts
swelling under her sweater..."
she imagined his thoughts
from his lingering gaze
over her, his later berating her
for being 'too moral'
when she stayed unresponsive
in his city office. Ironically
she'd gone there for therapy
after her hospital doctor
whom she cared for
had moved away.

And after her first year of law school
she applied for a summer internship
at the public interest group where
she used to work. The director hugged her,
and she smiled, then stiffened
when he said in a genial oblivious tone
"you don't mind
working on our benefit committee
instead of on legal issues, do you?"

Recently her lovely grown daughter said
she'd been harassed at work for years
by most of her bosses, and she wondered
if anything had changed since 1991
when Anita Hill testified on her past
harassment by Supreme Court nominee
Clarence Thomas, who prevailed,
the way Trump prevailed as president
after bragging about grabbing
women by the ass and worse.

IV. EYE

Time in Music

tardo
        as a child, offered lessons
        in piano, then cello,
        I didn't learn to read
        the notes for either
        nor how to keep time
        with the metronome's beat
        so practiced neither.
        Instead, on summer afternoons
        I'd swing in a hammock, gazing
        at shafts of late sun
        moving slowly, with time
        slowing   too

allegro
        with my own children's birth
        life became a glad fast dance,
        and so with less time
        I focused more
        on finding the notes
        to draw the bow
        of my cello over the strings,
        but keeping the meter
        seemed a mathematician's feat
        still beyond my reach.

presto
        the world pressed in:
        Three Mile Island, Indian Point,
        Columbine, Sandy Hook
        meetings, protests, marches
        hurry hurry hurry
        no time for music, art, poetry.

adagio
   now my pace is slow, at ease
   but sometimes, sinking in bed
   and staring at darkness, I hear
   my heart beating, and wonder
   in fear what time will bring, until
   I listen to Chopin's fluid cascading notes
   or Scott Joplin's syncopating rhythms
   and I float suspended, beyond time.

Windscape

Light moving over hills
across a bone-white river
over a sere ochre field
with indigo shadows
through flamelike forms of trees
tossed by an unseen wind—
a windscape Hongnian paints
with mauve, russet,
sienna, orange, scarlet
pigments on a small canvas
he's arranged his palette
in complementary hues
of orange and blue:
scarlet, orange, deep yellow;
blue-violet, cobalt, phthalo turquoise
with softer tones of indigo
and burnt sienna. "Catch the light
before the shadows shift"
he tells us, "then cover your large canvas
quickly, thickly
with the light *yang* pattern;
paint the shadows quickly, thinly
in the dark *yin* pattern."
He murmurs: "Lighter, darker,
warmer, cooler, brighter, softer"
as he covers his canvas
with swift soft brushstrokes.
"And look for the *chi*,"
he says, "the hidden dragon
moving through your painting."
I watch him work, and see
the tortion of the invisible wind
tossing the treetops, rippling the river,
the *chi*, the hidden dragon
twisting through his painting.

Sense and Spirit
> *"What is the thing that lies beneath the semblance of the thing?"*
> from *The Waves,* by Virginia Woolf

I gather things for a still life:
pear, egg, vase, mushrooms
and set up my easel, canvas, palette,
twist off the caps of my pigments
and squeeze them from their tubes:
alizarin, burnt sienna, quinacridone among the reds;
cerulean, cobalt, ultramarine in the blues;
cadmium, ochre, raw sienna among the yellows.
I feel the oily thickness in the bristles of my brushes,
smell the sharp-acrid, sweet-oily aromas
of turpentine and linseed oil
as I mix more pigments, press and swirl them
onto the rough weave of my canvas
and paint: lost, absorbed, at peace.

At the end of the afternoon
I scrape the pigments from my palette,
look at my canvas, and wonder
if the egg, pear, vase, and mushrooms
I've painted are like
the real ones on the table,
or *only* like them, or whether
I've been able to impart
something—I grasp for a word
that's not corny or inadequate—
of their essence, soul or heart.

I hold in my hands the egg and pear,
aware of their different hefts,
clean the rounded cap of a cremini mushroom
with a mushroom brush, letting the sound
'mushroom brush' swish and sift through me.

I know these things mostly
through their hues, shapes, or the sound
of their names, and I wonder
at the absurdity of words
with their similar sounds:

pear, pare, pair, peer,
and different meanings: sole, soul—
(sole of a shoe, sole as a fish,
sole in the sense of only)
and soul as one's sole unique essence—
words' similar sounds, but their meanings
remain a mystery, metaphors or similes
seem futile: to the outward eye
"a rose is a rose is a rose"
more than bread is flesh, or wine is blood,
and a woman's eyes may shine like the sun
for one lover, while for another
his "Mistress' eyes are nothing like the sun."

One week the leader of our Meditation group
prefaces our practice with a new video
of a priest praising "centering prayer
as the source of the Indwelling Trinity:
Father, Son, and Holy Spirit."
'Indwelling?' This sounds like the 'influx'
of spirit corresponding to the senses
invoked by Blake in his mystical poems,
and by Inness in his mystical paintings.

The lights are dimmed, a candle lit
as we sit in a circle. I gaze at the flame
and focus on my favorite image:
the majestic maple tree near our house.
This time I dutifully try to visualize
God the Father in the roots,
Christ the Son in the massive trunk,
the Holy Spirit in the spreading branches.

But something in me pushes back: why
should I construct a tortuous comparison—
especially with the implication that not only
the Father and Son are male,
but also the Holy Spirit?

I'd rather imagine

31

the tree itself, with its stark
seal-brown bark in winter, its feathery
citrine-green leaves in spring, its full
thick foliage in summer. And its flaming
leaves in autumn, whose orange-scarlet,
saffron, and russet hues I paint
feeling by this I am praising the earth
and wanting to worship Gaia as Mother Earth
or Sophia as Wisdom, or diverse
female voices in gnostic poems:
"I am androgynous. I am both
Mother and Father", or the female voice
in the gnostic poem "The Thunder"
that delights in paradox:
"I am the name of the sound
and the sound of the name"

as I look at the tree, then at my canvas
with the sense of a spirit-like current running
from the leaves to my eyes,
hand, brushes, pigments, painting.

Remembered Landscapes

Brittle Winter

    knot beds' circular enigmas
    in my father's garden
    crusted with rime, enclosed
    by yews, dusted with snow;
    arbor vitae lining long allées,
    all held by a curve of stone wall
    like an arched eyebrow
    leading out to a field with
    stubs of dun dry cornstalks
    pocking the pale cheek
    of cornfield, creased
    with furrows, edged by lines
    of green-black pines,
    below saffron clouds
    of willow boughs
    fading into far violet hills—
    manuscript etched calligraphic:
    sepia branches starkly marked
    on glistening parchment snow;
    husks of stalks rattling in icy wind,
    while far below, cotyledons
    of embryonic leaves
    unfurl from seeds,
    dormant, unfolding.

City Spring

    tiny threads of citrine
    threaded on thin green
    grass blades growing from clefts
    of jagged rocks glinting with mica
    near paths in the park
    where my sister and I play
    hopscotch, jump-rope, roller skate
    all afternoon, until we turn back
    to our mother's apartment
    stacked above others
    in this gritty,
    wretched, exhilarating
    city

Summer Ocean
    dry sand
    burning our bare feet
    as S and I
    walk past the boat shed
    with its worn grey wood,
    past the long brackish pond
    fringed with reeds
    and marsh rose mallows,
    past tall thickets
    of coppery bayberry bushes
    curving around a bend
    up to a ridge, with
    the thick sweet stench
    of mud and underbrush
    suddenly turning
    into the sharp
    stiff tang of salt air
    as we stand on a dune
    hearing the pulsing thud
    of waves, and far
    beyond,
    the muffled, tonic roar
    of the wide, blue, surging
    ocean.

Autumn Anchor
    asters, goldenrod, glistening bronze
    burning bush, rising in tangled branches
    on banks of the brown-green stream
    flowing slowly
    through farm fields, down
    from hills blazoned
    with firs, oaks, maples,
    the stream now quickening, cutting
    through rock, above a path
    winding with pine trees,
    the torrent now plunging
    into a chasm, then eddying
    around a mossy, tree-shadowed

islet at the mouth of the river.
And walking down the path
to the small promontory
with a jutting hemlock,
I can feel my restless heart becoming
rested, rooted,
anchored
in an all-seasons mooring,
anchorite like the great
blue heron whose wide
slate-blue wings I watch
slowly lift and soar
into the sky, beyond the sedge
and flaming leaves of the euonymus bush
at the river's edge.

Elizabeth Shafer is an artist, writer, and lawyer.

As an artist, she does mostly oil paintings, although she also works in other media like printmaking and encaustics. She has studied at the Art Students' League, the Woodstock School of Art, and R& F. Encaustics Studios. She has exhibited at Emerge Gallery in Saugerties, N.Y., and has had a solo art exhibit at the Saugerties Public Library during May and June 2019.

As an author, she writes poetry, fiction, and non-fiction. For the latter, she has focused on the legal obligation to negotiate in good faith toward the total abolition of nuclear weapons. She has taken courses at the Unterberg Poetry Center of the 92nd Street Y and at the Gotham Writers Workshops. She was a Contributor in Fiction in 2014, and a Contributor in Poetry in 2015, at the Bread Loaf Writers Conferences.

As a lawyer, she is involved in environmental and international humanitarian issues. Since 1991 she has been a Board Member of the Lawyers' Committee on Nuclear Policy.